Instructor's Guide

VIEWPOINTS

READINGS WORTH THINKING AND WRITING ABOUT

W. Royce Adams
Santa Barbara City College, Emeritus
and
Maggie Barbieri

FIFTH EDITION

HOUGHTON MIFFLIN COMPANY BOSTON NEW YORK

Senior Sponsoring Editor: Mary Jo Southern
Development Editor: Kellie Cardone
Manufacturing Manager: Florence Cadran
Marketing Manager: Annamarie Rice
Editorial Assistant: Peter Mooney

Printed in the U.S.A.

ISBN: 0-618-31846-1

1 2 3 4 5 6 7 8 9—QT—07 06 05 04 03

CONTENTS

INTRODUCTION

This *Instructor's Guide* offers some suggestions for users of *Viewpoints: Readings Worth Thinking and Writing About,* Third Edition. Recommendations for assigning and helping students get the most from "Part I: Viewpoints on Reading and Writing Essays" appear here, along with commentaries on each of the reading selections in "Part II: Readings Worth Thinking and Writing About." These comments may help you decide which readings you wish to assign during the course and in which order.

The reading selections in *Viewpoints* have not been selected as "models" of excellent writing that students must then try to emulate. The selections are end products and do not reflect the multitude of changes the authors may have gone through. Instead, the selections were chosen for the stimulation of thought they may stir in the student. Some readings are very well written, others are not. Your task is to show students why some authors do a better job than others. In that capacity, then, the readings can serve as "models." Thought, I believe, should come before concern for a rhetorical mode, and all the readings were selected because they provide students with various viewpoints on a topic they must ultimately think about before they express their own minds in writing.

Throughout this guide, you'll read frequent suggestions that call for small group or class discussions. While such an emphasis may seem strange in a book dealing with composition, my experience has shown that lively class discussions and a controlled exchange of viewpoints stimulate student thinking, thus effecting thoughtful student compositions by the end of the term.

I strongly recommend that you have students keep a reading journal in which they write their reactions to essays and their answers to the questions for the readings you assign. Encourage them to write down any questions or problems they have regarding selections so that they can bring them to class for clarification. Let them know that capturing their initial thoughts as they read as well as after is important and could ultimately lead to a topic for an essay of their own. You may also want them to use their journals for keeping a record of the vocabulary words taken from the readings that they need to learn.

As you read through this *Guide,* you may notice some redundant comments. It seems unavoidable. Remarks made for one reading selection or unit may also apply to another, and since instructors will no doubt skip around in the text or omit certain readings from their course syllabus, repetition of some suggestions has to occur.

All the approaches presented here have worked for me, but they are never meant as the way you should use the book. My hope is that *Viewpoints* is designed so that all users find it compatible with their own teaching styles.

RATIONALE FOR PART I

Many years of teaching freshman composition have led me to believe that most students lack the necessary analytical skills required to read and react to assigned readings as we would like. In addition, many students have little or no understanding of the writing process or what good writing entails. Since one of the goals of *Viewpoints* is to teach the interrelationship of reading and writing skills, Part I is divided into two chapters for this purpose. Chapter 1 teaches students how to read essays; Chapter 2 teaches how to write them. Every effort has been made to show how these two basic skills complement one another.

For some students, Chapter 1 serves as an introduction and for others a review of such fundamentals as the essay structure, the difference between a topic and a thesis, paragraph patterns or modes used for developing topic sentences, and transitional devices required of certain patterns. The same fundamentals presented when teaching composition are presented here as tools for better reading comprehension. In addition, Chapter 1 shows students how to separate main ideas from supporting details, how to distinguish fact from opinion, and how to draw inferences. These reading skills are, of course, the same skills a writer must consider when composing. Finally, ways to retain comprehension through notetaking, textbook marking, and journal keeping are explained and encouraged. In effect, Chapter 1 is a minicourse on how to read analytically with frequent references to the writing connection.

Chapter 2 builds on the content of Chapter 1 by showing how the methods and qualities of a good essay reader can be applied to essay writing. The chapter provides the student with what are generally accepted as the three basic writing stages: prewriting, writing, and rewriting. Again, this chapter serves as an introduction or a review of the writing process, continually reminding students that writing is a recursive process.

My experience has been that many freshman students need a sense of direction, an example to follow in order to get started on safe ground. Chapter 2 does this by taking students through the entire writing process, showing them how someone might begin an essay and work through several revisions before arriving at a final draft. In so doing, students are taken step by step through prewriting techniques (such as using questions or reactions from their reading journals, brainstorming, clustering, and freewriting), to writing techniques (such as discovering a working thesis, developing and organizing support, and writing a first draft), to revising techniques, including editing and proofreading. The text points out, as you will no doubt wish to do, that there are as many ways to approach writing as there are writers, and that students must discover what works best for them.

Part I, then, provides a background and a useful resource for students that establishes a sense of direction and an understanding of what is expected of them when they are assigned the readings in Part II and the writing of full-length compositions.

Using Chapter 1: Viewpoints on Reading Essays

Chapter 1 supplies students with the analytical reading skills necessary for reading the essays in *Viewpoints* as well as other sources by teaching them what an essay is, how it is structured, how to read with greater comprehension, and how to retain and use an essay's content. For this reason, I recommend that Chapter 1 be assigned the first week of class.

The Writing Exercises Interspersed with the discussion of reading to understand topic, thesis, supporting evidence, paragraph patterns, and order of support are opportunities for students to interact by responding to questions that test their understanding. Because these questions are followed by explanatory answers, it is possible to assign all or parts of Chapter 1 for out-of-class reading. However, in order to monitor students' comprehension of this information, three brief writing exercises have been provided at appropriate intervals. Rather than assigning the entire chapter at once, you may prefer to use the writing exercises as a breaking point for three separate assignments. This would depend on the ability of the class and how thoroughly you want to cover this chapter.

These three writing exercises can be used in several ways. On the one hand, you can use them as diagnostic tools, a means to discover the strengths and weaknesses of the class so that you have some idea what skill areas need more coverage than others. On the other hand, you may prefer that students return all three for grading, as an assurance before moving on that the material has been understood. The results of the paragraph writings may reveal a need to go over all or parts of the chapter in class, or they may reflect that the class is ready for Chapter 2. Another approach is to use the exercises as "pop" quizzes, surprising the students to see if they did read and understand the assignment. Or, as the students work through the chapter, have them write the three exercises in their reading journals. You then can read them during a later journal check.

The Reading Journal You'll notice that I encourage students to keep a reading journal. The chapter emphasizes why and how to write summaries of assigned readings, the need for recording any personal reflections after reading, and the maintenance of a vocabulary list for study. Reading and journal keeping may not be an approach you wish your students to take; if so, mention it as something they may want to do on their own if they feel it will help them. However, it *will* help them, and I strongly recommend that students be required to maintain a reading journal, at least in part. If journal keeping is done correctly, students become more actively involved in the reading process. You can modify the journal assignments by selecting certain readings for which you want entries, rather than requiring entries for all assigned readings. The reading journal can also be used for other items for which you wish a student response, such as writing answers to any of the questions that follow the reading selections freewriting, or in-class writing practices.

Marking Notes in the Text Another reason for assigning Chapter 1 first is that it illustrates for students how to separate main ideas from supporting details, how to separate facts from opinions, and how to draw inferences. Students are also shown how to read with pen in hand, to make thoughtful notations, and to have a dialogue with the author as they read. This information lays the groundwork for careful reading of all the assigned selections in Chapter 2.

Even though students are provided with practice in marking up Pete Hamill's essay, "The Wet Drug" (page 29), it might be efficacious during the first or second week to select one or two essays from any chapter in Part II for additional practice of the skills taught in Chapter 1. Since the chapters do not have to be read in any order, you could, for example, assign Christy Haubegger's "The Legacy of Generation Ñ" and Leonard Pitts, "Your Kid's Going to Pay for Cheating—Eventually." They are distinctly different in structure, tone, and language. Haubegger's piece is written in a style that combines personal opinion with argument-supporting statistics and examples, while Pitts takes on the issue of plagiarism by telling a story which uses short, powerful paragraphs that give evidence to how he feels about the people about whom he writes. You may want to point out that some of the selections are short stories and poems, requiring a different reading approach from essays.

Pointing out these differences, discussing thesis and its location or implication, main ideas and supporting details, implied statements, facts versus opinion, and so on, would aid students when called upon to read on their own. Such an approach would reveal some of the range and diversity of authors and point up the need for analytical reading comprehension.

Initially, students need to be shown how to read and mark assigned reading selections. I've found it's helpful and fun to read certain passages from the readings aloud, providing the necessary tone and attitude students must learn to provide for themselves when reading silently. We can't assume that students know how to read the way we want them to read; thus, we must show them. Only then can we begin to use the readings as a means for exposing them to humanistic ideas and the range of viewpoints that exist on many topics.

Some students are reluctant to mark up their textbooks, but I show them how one of my books looks after I've read and reacted to an author. I try to convince them, as Mortimer Adler does so well in his classic "How to Mark a Book," that the benefits of marking up a book far outweigh any price they may receive during the campus bookstore buy-back period. I share with them the Herman Ebbinghaus "curve of forgetting" that appears in most freshman psychology textbooks, which reveals how quickly we forget what we learn if we don't reinforce our memory (over 40 percent within twenty minutes, over 55 percent in one hour, and around 70 percent after nine hours).

If you have students keep a reading journal, you may want them to share their entries either in small groups or with the entire class. Students will see that not everyone responds to a selection the same way, nor comprehends the same meaning. This serves to make clear that some reading selections require more than one reading, and that through exchange of thoughtful discussions, most everyone can eventually come to an agreement on what an author's thesis is, without necessarily agreeing with the viewpoint.

I contend that the time spent dealing with the reading skills taught in Chapter 1 will result in better student compositions. My recommendation is that you don't assign any full-length essays until after you have covered both Chapters 1 and 2.

Using Chapter 2: Viewpoints on Writing Essays

Don't assign Chapter 2 until at least a week has been spent on Chapter 1 and after the class has undertaken a close examination of two or three selected essays in Part II. Rather than leaving students on their own, it seems best to make certain they have some guided practice applying the skills taught in Chapter 1. At least the same amount of time should be given to Chapter 2, depending upon the level of your students. Obviously, some classes may require more time, some less.

There are four writing exercises, similar to those in Chapter 1, appearing periodically after specific information on composition has been presented. The exercises call for a written application or a summary of the material read. You may want to use these exercises as a way to divide the chapter into four separate assignments, each one followed by the completion of the writing exercise. As in Chapter 1, these exercises can be graded, used as quizzes, or assigned as journal entries. I favor collecting them so that student comprehension can be monitored, using them as a gauge for the amount of time needed to be spent on the chapter. These exercises also serve as an indicator of which students are keeping up with the assignments.

The Prewriting Activities While many prewriting heuristics exist, three rather universally accepted ones are presented for students in *Viewpoints:* reacting to questions and statements from the readings recorded in their journals, brainstorming (listing and clustering), and freewriting. (If you are unfamiliar with freewriting and clustering as prewriting activities, Peter Elbow's *Writing with Power,* Oxford Press, 1978, and Gabriele Lusser Rico's *Writing the Natural Way,* J.P. Tarcher, 1983, are highly recommended.) Once presented with various prewriting methods, students seem to favor one of these three approaches.

It's been my experience that students need practice in prewriting beyond what they get in the text. Take the time to do some prewriting board work in class. For instance, I ask students to give me a topic, any topic, which I then write on the board. Next, I ask them to provide some possible working theses based on the topic. This activity helps clarify the difference between a topic and a thesis, plus reveals for them the wide range of directions one can take on any given subject. Then I ask students to provide some ideas or supporting evidence that can be used to support one of the thesis statements we formulate together. Sometimes we brainstorm, sometimes we cluster. When thoughts are exhausted or time infringes, we look over our list or clusters, erasing those points that fail to relate to the thesis. I can never anticipate what the results will be any more than the students can. Together we discover what will work and what won't. The students thus take part in the prewriting stage and learn what is expected of them when given their first full-length essay writing assignment.

Follow this type of board work with the next phase, organizing those ideas left on the board that relate to the thesis. Students learn that there is a variety of ways to organize supporting evidence for an essay and that it may take several drafts to figure out which approach reads best. After such a class activity, I call their attention to pages 47–52 to show the parallel between what we've done on the board and the example in the text itself.

Whatever way it is done, the teaching of prewriting activities is an invaluable lesson. Practices in one or more of these prewriting exercises before assigning full-length essays benefit both the student and you when the full-length composition is finally assigned.

The Nutshell Statement You may not want to require students to complete a nutshell statement as described on pages 54–56 in the text. However, I find it helpful to them and to me when I require that one be attached to every essay, at least during the early stage of the course. When I have individual conferences with students, I use the nutshell statements to point out where their strengths and weaknesses are in relation to their purpose (thesis), support (organization and logic), and audience (tone and style). Once students are writing well enough, I no longer require the nutshell statement unless they find it helpful.

If you do want to use nutshells, you will probably find that students need some help in preparing ones that are not vague or hurriedly written. Sometimes I distribute handouts with examples of nutshell statements from previous students' work. I usually share in class both good and bad student examples without identifying the authors.

I frequently ask students to write a nutshell statement for one of the reading selections in the text as a writing assignment. Sharing their written nutshells in class leads to interesting discussions of the assigned reading, often revealing biases and discrepancies in their comprehension of the reading selection. It is also revealing to have students exchange their own essays, requesting that classmates write nutshell statements for comparison with the student author's, showing the students how others perceive their work and making them aware that the instructor is not the only audience for whom they are writing.

Make certain that students don't use their nutshell statements as their opening paragraphs. Students should understand that the nutshell statement itself is not a part of their essay.

Paragraph Patterns The information on rhetorical modes on pages 57–60 should be compared with that on pages 8–16 in Chapter 1. It serves as a reinforcement of the reading-writing connection.

I find it rather artificial to ask students to write using a particular rhetorical mode. It seems to place the pattern before thought and content. After students write a rough draft, I then ask them to see if some pattern appeared naturally. When they revise, I remind them they may need to express their thoughts using a different pattern. Still, there may be a place for requesting that students use a particular paragraph pattern as a drill or an exercise in understanding that pattern.

You may want to select examples of various modes reflected in paragraphs from essays in Part II as models to share in class. See the Rhetorical Table of Contents in the student text for a classification of essays according to the various rhetorical paragraph modes found within the readings.

Viewpoints approaches the use of paragraph patterns as a way to develop information based on the way a topic sentence is written. The text itself says all that need be said here.

The Student Model Essay It's worth class time to look carefully at the various drafts of the model student essay on pages 61–75 as a way to discuss recursive writing. Point out the various changes from draft to draft, stressing the importance of revision. Although the text visually illustrates these changes, it is recommended that you make certain through class discussion that students see and understand the changes and additions that were made. Many students will not actually notice some of the changes unless they are pointed out.

The student model essay offers an opportunity to emphasize the need for revision, but it also provides you with a tool for discussing how you would respond to and grade the essay, and provides students with a better understanding of your own particular demands and expectations.

In addition to the model student essay in this chapter, there is one at the end of every chapter in Part II. Some are well written, some flawed. I think students can learn from the mistakes that appear in the essays as well as from the positive aspects. Obviously, your comments may often disagree with mine.

The Revising and Editing Checklists You will probably want to discuss in class the checklists provided to help clarify any terminology or points students don't understand. The checklists are of little value if the students can't interpret what they are meant to check.

Brief versions of the expanded revising and editing checklists are provided at the end of Chapter 2 for the convenience of the student. You can request that the students apply these checklists to each of their essays before they submit their work to you.

RATIONALE FOR PART II

The eight chapters that comprise Part II fulfill several of this book's objectives. The readings provide a variety of viewpoints, thematically arranged, on contemporary issues with four types of follow-up questions that stimulate or suggest to students ideas for their own essays; they contain a wide range of examples of professional and student writing; and they directly or indirectly offer possibilities for simple research projects. The chapters can be read in any order, and, if you wish, you can skip around through the chapters ignoring the themes altogether. Having more essays in the book than you will have time to cover during the course allows you to choose only the selections you want to assign or use in class.

Each chapter contains a broad theme with which all students will have some familiarity. Before assigning essays from any chapter, spend some class time and attention on the photos, "Focus on . . ." sections, and short prefatory comments that open each chapter. They introduce the chapter's theme and help focus student attention on the chapter readings. For instance, the prefatory comments for Chapter 4 explain how social scientists, sociologists, psychologists, and economists define human behavior. You can remind students that their textbooks from these classes might contain a wealth of stimulation for an essay or possible research paper. Students will begin to see that ideas for essays don't have to come from among those suggested in the book, that there is a connection between the English course they are taking and the "real world."

Many students often have difficulty concentrating on assigned readings unless the subject truly interests them. As a way to prepare students for a reading assignment, prereading questions require a brief survey of the selection and a prediction about the content. The questions are based on two well-known reading techniques, the DRTA (Directed Reading-Thinking Activity) and the first steps of the SQ3R (Survey, Question, Read, Recite, Review). Requiring students to answer these prereading questions forces them to concentrate on what they are about to read. Just as a camera must be focused before taking a picture, the reader must focus on what is about to be read. Remind students that the prereading questions are part of each reading assignment. In fact, you may want to go over the prereading questions with the students at the time you assign the reading selection, a sort of preview of coming attractions.

A list of key vocabulary words provided before the selection itself permits students to preview the definitions and note the essay paragraphs where the words appear. Some instructors like to discuss these words with the students at the time the reading assignment is given. Others prefer to deal with vocabulary after students have read the piece. Still others leave the learning of vocabulary up to the individual student. I like to go over the words with the students when I assign the essay, answering any questions they may have and assuring correct pronunciation. It seems to make the reading of the essay easier for them.

The four sets of questions that follow each reading selection reinforce the skills presented in Part I. The first set, **Understanding the Content,** deals with basic comprehension elements: recognizing thesis, main ideas, supporting evidence, fact and opinion, and so on. They are questions for which answers can usually be agreed upon. The next set, **Looking at Structure and Style,** focuses on the author's organization, paragraph patterns, language usage, transitional techniques, and the like: in effect, most of the composition fundamentals taught in Chapter 2. The third set of questions, **Evaluating the Author's Viewpoints,** calls for personal reactions, critical thinking, and evaluation of what was read. **Pursuing Possible Essay Topics,** the last set, offers a variety of ideas or starting points for student essays or research projects dealing with the chapter's theme.

The first three sets of questions can be used in several ways. Some can be selected for reading journal entries, some for class discussion, others for "pop" quizzes. Some instructors like to break the class into small groups, making each group responsible for providing answers to specific questions, or to assign individuals specific questions to answer orally in class. More ways to use the questions are mentioned later in this guide when individual essays are discussed.

For those instructors introducing their students to the research project, the fourth set of questions frequently contains suggestions that require more reading. Some of the items offer specific book titles or library sources for students to pursue. You may want to divide your class into groups, assigning students to pursue. You may want to divide your class into groups, assigning each group one of the questions to brainstorm or discuss, then have the students share their ideas with the entire class.

Part II provides more than enough reading selections for a one-term course. The intentional abundance and diversity of style and difficulty allow you to choose the readings most appropriate for the level of your class and the length of your course. I have found that students often can, if interested in the subject, read above their expected level. Don't let a seemingly difficult selection deter you from assigning it. If they are to develop their skills, students need the challenge of more difficult reading. The intent is to provide instructors with interesting material useful in teaching students how to read and write at a higher level than they could handle when they entered the class. Good instruction requires students to be challenged, not just fed easy material because they are "under prepared." How else will they ever get prepared?

Using Chapter 3: Viewpoints on Learning

While it is not necessary to begin with this chapter after finishing Part I, doing so can be useful because most students at this point in the course are experiencing a new kind of learning adaptation to college life. If you are assigning essay topics on themes, learning is an appropriate starting place. Discussing in class the "Focus on . . ." questions and prefatory materials focuses students on the broad theme of learning and prepares them for any of the essays you assign.

When assigning a reading selection, periodically remind students of the reading skills taught in Chapter 1. Go over the prereading questions and vocabulary words with the students. You may want to look at some of the words in context as part of a prereading activity. Although it may not be practical to do this with every reading assignment, it helps to do this with the more difficult reading selections.

Following are some comments and suggestions for using the essays in this chapter.

"To Err Is Wrong" by Roger von Oech

If you can't assign all of the essays in this chapter, this is not one to skip. The subject of failure and success is on the minds of most students—indeed, most all of us. The idea that failure can bring success is important, especially to student writers who struggle with the fear of failure or live with their past failure. I recommend at least reading paragraph 26 aloud and discussing the four tips in class.

In paragraph 8, von Oech quotes the baseball player Yaz, "If you want hits, be prepared for misses," and equates this comment to the way the game of life goes. Remind students that that's also the way writing an essay goes—lots of false starts, lots of errors, lots of revisions before that successful final draft. Emphasize that errors can be stepping stones to success.

Because of the variety of paragraph patterns used—cause/effect, comparison/contrast, examples, use of anecdote—the selection can be used to discuss and reinforce rhetorical modes. The questions under "Looking at Structure and Style" provide for such an approach. As an aside, you might want to point out the difference in handling a lengthy quotation (the block quote in paragraph 17) and in citing shorter quotations (those in paragraphs 11 and 19).

"In Praise of the F Word" by Mary Sherry

This essay raises the issues of the grading system, attitudes toward learning, teacher competency, parental responsibility, and the levels of literacy, all good topics for possible essays. Ask students to form groups and discuss their various learning experiences. Have them argue for or against grades or one of the issues mentioned above. You could use this piece as a way to discuss an argumentative essay: What is Sherry's thesis? Is it supported with sound arguments? What are they? What's wrong with her argument? Would she feel this way if her son hadn't been threatened with an F?—and so on.

Sherry says, "Passing students who have not mastered the work cheats them and the employers who expect graduates to have basic skills," a statement that usually provokes discussion. Many of my students have this complaint. "Why was I passed on? Why wasn't I made to learn? I'm in this class because I wasn't taught the skills I needed." I'm certain you have your own favorite retorts to their anger and excuses for not learning, which leads to some lively class discussions.

Take time to discuss all the questions under "Looking at Structure and Style."

"Your Kid's Going to Pay for Cheating--Eventually" by Leonard Pitts

It would seem that plagiarism is the topic of this selection. However, the real issue here concerns students, their parents, and a set of behaviors that contributed to one teacher's resignation in a Kansas school district. See if students understand what is really at issue here: students clearly plagiarizing their work and their parents contention that they had done nothing wrong.

Students are probably aware of what constitutes "cheating" in its most literal sense. But, like the students and their parents in this selection, they may not be aware of what constitutes "plagiarism." You can start the discussion by asking students for a definition of plagiarism and then go on to point out what constitutes plagiarism, using some of the most recent cases related to professional writers such as Doris Kearns Goodwin and others. Although we might think of plagiarism as a black and white issue, the definition of the word may vary in the students' minds. Students can be sent to one of the many sites that deal with plagiarism to test their own definition of the word. By going to "Turnitin.com" with one of their own papers and submitting it, they can see if their definition of plagiarism is the same as the one presented on a professional web site devoted to the subject. They will also be able to see if anything they have used in any of their research papers qualifies as being too close to someone else's work.

Leonard Pitts' tone in this piece and his attitude toward the subject of the cheating, the students, and their parents is evident from the first few paragraphs. Ask students to pick out those words and/or phrases that indicate how Pitts feels about the parents, students, and Christine Pelton. Do students think that the parents were correct in supporting their children? Or, do they agree that the situation presented by Pitts was morally reprehensible, given the circumstances?

Also, ask students what they would have done if they were a) the students in the story (would they have admitted to wrongdoing?), b) a parent of one of the students accused of plagiarism (would they have defended their child or punished them?) or c) Christine Pelton (would they have taken a stand, as she did?)

"Essence of Education" by Robert W. Tracinski

Tracinski is a senior writer for the Ayn Rand Institute, which according to its web site is "the center for the advancement of Objectivism, Ayn Rand's philosophy of reason, egoism, individualism, and laissez-faire capitalism." This selection may result in spirited class discussion, depending on the mix of students you have, their experience and knowledge of the subject of creationism, and their individual opinions regarding the subject. It would be helpful to get a sense of where students stand (if they have an opinion at all) on this issue prior to their reading of the selection so that you can be prepared for the type of discussion that will ensue.

The author takes a decidedly anti-Creationism stance and presents what could be perceived as controversial statements in the selection. For instance, ask your students what they think of the question raised in paragraph 10, "If the Creationist approach were taken seriously, what would remain of education?"

This selection provides the perfect opportunity to have students work on an opinion paper, as suggested in some of the writing prompts given in the "Pursuing Possible Essay Topics" section at the end of the question set.

"The Practicality of the Liberal Arts Major" by Debra Sikes and Barbara Murray

Even though the authors intended this essay for college teachers, students will find this essay interesting because it reflects what research has discovered about the practicality of the liberal arts degree. Paragraph 5 discusses where and what the research project was about. Paragraph 7 shows the skills, in order of importance, that a college student should acquire for future jobs. Paragraph 8 provides the authors' recommendations to students based on their findings.

It can be a useful essay for getting students to rethink their college goals. You might want to call their attention to the key points in paragraphs 7 and 8. Ask them if they are presently taking or planning to take the courses that will benefit them the most. Do they believe it is possible to be "overeducated"? Such questions get students to see that the reading selection can and does relate to them personally.

Good follow-up writing drills and/or essay topics are numbers 2, 4, 5, and 6, as they direct the students to consider their reasons for attending college, their learning skills, and the benefits derived from a college education.

Calling attention to the stylistic differences between this and the Baker essay may prove valuable. Structure, as well as tone and attitude, are quite different.

"The Lesson" by Toni Cade Bambara

Toni Cade (who adopted the surname Bambara later in her life) was born in New York City and attended Queens College and City College. "The Lesson" is a rather lengthy selection and may prove difficult for some students. Encourage them to stick with the piece, looking up words when necessary, or rereading parts or all of the selection. This may help students understand the meaning of the selection or to get at some of the key points that will emerge from reading this piece of literature.

Students may or may not have trouble with the colloquial language used in the selection. It would be interesting to have a brief discussion of how the author's use of language helps to define each character.

It may be interesting to have the students identify which of the characters in the story they feel are most like themselves, or in whom they see the most similar character traits. Most students will be able to recognize traits or entire characters that remind them of themselves either in the present or when they were children.

The most important message in the selection can be found in paragraph 50 when Miss Moore asks the children, "Imagine for a minute what kind of society it is in which some people can spend on a toy what it would cost to feed a family of six or seven." See if students can identify this main point, and if so, get their reaction to this question. Further exploration of this question and other questions raised by the selection can be found in the "Evaluating the Author's Viewpoints" in the questions following "The Lesson."

"Vouchers Answer New Segregation in Our Schools" by Paul Goldman

Before discussing this particular essay, along with the Eichel essay that comes next, see if students understand what a school voucher is and why the issue of vouchers is such a contentious one. Students may or may not come to class with an opinion about school vouchers. Perhaps, before they read this and the following selection, you can distribute some information about the issue of vouchers in order to prepare them for a discussion of the topic.

You may also want to review what students know about civil rights in general, and "separate but equal" specifically. Are students aware that only fifty years ago, black children were still denied an equal education? Were they aware of the issue of busing and integration? What do they know, and how do they feel about these events in our history?

An interesting exercise might be to have students find out how their local or state representatives feel about the issue of school vouchers and why. They can go to the web or do research in the library in the periodicals section to find out this information. By doing this, students will have a better understanding of how this issue is divided along party lines and affects people's opinions at voting times.

Goldman writes with great fervor on this topic. Perhaps students can through the essay and pick out those words and phrases that illustrate how strongly the author feels about the topic.

Before going on to read the Eichel essay, which can be taught in tandem with this essay, see if students have come to a conclusion about school vouchers. Then, after reading Eichel, find out how many (if any at all) opinions have changed.

"School Vouchers Don't Seem the Answer" by Larry Eichel

Like the previous selection by Goldman, Eichel feels very strongly about this topic. Unlike Goldman, who gives some history for his opinion and that of the people he presents in his selection, Eichel stays very much in the present by focusing on Chief Justice Rehnquist and Clarence Thomas as majority opinions in the 5-4 Court ruling. Ask students if Goldman's style or presenting history in the context of his argument, or Eichel's remaining the present is more effective. Why do they feel the way they do?

Now that they have read both arguments on school vouchers, whose do they feel is more effective and why? How do individual students feel about vouchers? Why? Has anyone changed their opinion after reading the Eichel selection? Again, why?

Both of these essays, and the topic in general, offer ample opportunity to write an argumentative essay. See "Pursuing Possible Essay Topics" for ideas, or have students write to their local representative arguing for or against school vouchers.

STUDENT ESSAY: **"College Brings Alienation"** by John Gonzales

You might like to inquire how many of your students consider they are breaking their family and cultural molds. With some encouragement, you may find students of ethnic minorities willing to talk about their own struggles with education and alienation from their home environments. Ask students if they have set limits on their own learning for fear of losing a cultural identity.

Gonzales sees education clearly as a way to further the role of Latinos in American society. You can contrast this with the more limited goals often associated with the practical courses of learning chosen by his fellows. What are the aspirations of comfortably off, middle-class students, perhaps just the latest in several generations to go to college? It may be interesting to see if they share Gonzales's fears about today's society and his motivations.

Using Chapter 4: Viewpoints on Human Behavior

The theme of human behavior appears after the one on learning simply because it, too, is broad and familiar enough for students to relate to without much strain. Should you use the chapter theme for a full-length essay assignment, the chapter's introductory comments help reflect the wide explanations for human behavior frequently given in textbooks. You might remind students that if they are taking psychology, sociology, or anthropology courses, they are studying human behavior and may find ideas and sources for essay topics from their other textbooks and lectures as well as from this book.

The "Focus on . . ." at the beginning of the chapter can generate some humorous responses. You may suggest to students that they clip some "advice" columns, such as Ann Landers, and bring them to class to stimulate discussion of human behavior.

"Call Me Crazy, But I Have to Be Myself" by Mary Seymour

This reading was chosen because it presents a seemingly "normal" woman living in society with mental illness. So often, the mentally ill are presented in a most unflattering light, but Seymour's essay shows that someone with a mental illness—specifically bipolar disorder—can marry, have children, work, and generally live in society without being "detected."

This essay offers the opportunity for students to explore their own feelings about mental illness. Without getting too personal, discussion could center around what students know about bipolar disorder and if they know anyone living with the illness. If they don't know anyone, do they think that they could tell if someone was living with the disease, now that they have read this selection?

Under "Looking at Structure and Style, focus on questions 3-5. This will allow students to explore the concept of tone (#3), the author's intent (#4), and the use of examples (#5).

The author does a wonderful job of juxtaposing her everyday life ("Every morning I send my son to junior high school, put on professional garb and drive off to my job as alumni-magazine editor at a prep school, where I've worked for six years.") with her life as someone living with bipolar disorder ("Sometimes I wish I could sit at the lunch table and talk about lithium and Celexa instead of "Will and Grace."). Discuss the examples the author uses to show her everyday life with her life as a sufferer of bipolar disorder. How do these comparisons underscore the author's contention that "sometimes I feel like an impostor"? How do students think that the author's coworkers would feel if they knew about her condition? Would their experiences with her on a day-to-day basis outweigh any preconceived notions they might have about mental illness?

"Night Walker" by Brent Staples

Staples's opening paragraph is very well done—so well done, in fact, that after reading only the first sentence, one of the early reviewers of the *Viewpoints* manuscript said that she would not read or teach this essay. Staples, of course, deliberately leads us to think he is some sinister person, probably a rapist or murderer. But as we read on we learn as he did, "his unwieldy inheritance, the ability to alter public space" by just being a black man among fearful whites.

Have students deal especially with questions 2–6 under "Looking at Structure and Style." Some readers may find it overly descriptive, a good discussion point. All the questions under "Evaluating the Author's Viewpoints" create some lively discussions, especially item 3.

You might, if you have time, get students to do some nonlibrary research. Have them keep track for a week or two of the number of street violence episodes being reported on national and local television news, in daily papers, and in national news magazines. Is such news frequent? Can it create more fear than it deserves? Does it seem biased in presentation, as Staples suggests?

"I'm Not a Dork; I'm Ahead of Today's Fashions" by Alan Ehrenhalt

This is a relatively easy article taken from USA Today. This selection will provide an opportunity for students to have some fun discussing fashion, trends, and relationships. This discussion will be particularly effective if you have a wide age-range of students in your class—the older the students, the more likely they are to remember the fads and fashion trends that Ehrenhalt writes about in this humorous piece.

Ask students to think about the way they dressed even five years ago and ask them if they still wear the same types of clothes. Ask them what trends they have adopted into their own wardrobes in past years and if they would wear some of those things now. Why or why not? Have them identify one trend that was very popular in the not-so-distant past (e.g. long, baggy pants, or the wearing of sports jerseys as shirts) and ask them if they think that that trend will resurface in the near future. There are a great number of discussion topics that can be used in relation to this topic, and the humorous nature of this piece might provide a break from some of the more serious topics in the text. Have fun with the subject matter and see what develops.

Look particularly at the questions in "Looking at Structure and Style" to see if students can identify the argument the author is trying to make and if he makes that argument successfully. This selection also provides the perfect opportunity to have students write a personal response paper where they discuss their own feelings about fashion, trends, and personal style.

"On Holidays and How to Make Them Work"
by Nikki Giovanni

The title sets both theme and tone for this acerbic, but humorous essay. Giovanni's use of her own retail experience and her identity as a Black American give the writing an edge, boosted by her direct, colloquial style. Ask if any students have worked holiday shifts and can contribute more sorry consumer stories. Be sure that students pick up on the ironic touches peppered throughout and the more subtle questions about race that underlie the author's wry depiction of sale promotions generating wannabe-blacks.

If possible, set this essay close to a national holiday to prompt a survey of the language and style of American sales literature parodied so well by the writer. On a more serious note, ask students of non-American backgrounds how Giovanni's picture of human behavior regarding national days contrasts with the national holiday activities of other countries. Can U.S. history majors bring some background? For example, states would only ratify the national constitution when they were allowed to substitute "the pursuit of happiness" with "the acquisition and protection of property" in their own versions!

"Sunday in the Park" by Bel Kaufman

There are strong, almost too obvious, psychological, gender, and class dynamics for students to chew on here, such as the wife's initial security at her husband's side, the contrast of the men's reading material, and the physical appearance of the two boys. The wife's shift in feeling, first articulated by her misdirected statement "I'm ashamed of you!" is the author's central focus, but each character's implied background, self-perception, and expectations could provide ample material for exploration in essay form. Ask students how the incident itself could be used as evidence for a range of themes and what other information would be needed to build a complete essay.

Description sets the tone in Kaufman's story, but dialogue, internal as well as external, drives it to a hard-hitting conclusion. The frustration of articulate, intellectual powers is a major subject here, a good starting point for a discussion on the nature of sarcasm as the wife's final, impulsive reaction, and, indeed, the general topic of "defeat of reason by force."

"**We Real Cool**" by Gwendolyn Brooks

How much human behavior can students discover in this short and deceptively simple piece? Here is expert encapsulation and distillation showing language in high gear, and the importance of rereading.

The title is a true hook, implying at once ethnicity, attitude, and education. It could even fire in the direction of the nineties debate on "ebonics." The first two lines are set as a subtitle with classical overtones, as if naming a painted tableau, its subject frozen in time: lucky seven or seven deadly sins. And there is no golden fleece, only grave digging. Truncated lines convey truncated education and lives, finding expression only in monosyllabic chant. The primitive peer group power of "We" leads inexorably to death, alone and isolated.

Do students catch the implicit violence of "Strike straight," the criminality, as well as consumption of thinning gin, and the sexual implications of jazzing June with its classical reference to Juno, goddess of love? Gwendolyn Brooks describes behavior as much an element of today's society as it was in Chicago's South Side of the forties and fifties. What does her rich, black perspective convey that a full-length essay could not and vice versa? Does one inspire student writing more than the other?

"**'The Ghetto Made Me Do It'**" by Francis Flaherty

The increasing prevalence of legal defenses seeking to absolve perpetrators from responsibility for their crimes often produces some gut reactions (and jokes) about lawyers. With Flaherty's essay, students have an opportunity to really look at the issues raised, but also to go beyond them.

Ask students if they expected a resolution to the legal dilemmas set out here. You can point out how the author uses a combination of patterns to weave in one direction, then to punch home her point from another. The author analyzes the arguments, but deliberately leaves them balanced and unresolved. Returning to horrifying graphic example in the conclusion, attention is refocused away from legal debate as secondary to the larger, underlying social issue.

The topics of the arguments presented are excellent starting points for students to explore further, from violence as a norm to bias against the poor in American justice. When would they feel someone could be excused from personal responsibility for a criminal act? See how they answer the wide-ranging questions of the final paragraph, the basis alone for some interesting essays.

For comparison of subject matter and stylistic treatment, try setting this piece to read in conjunction with Toufexis's "Seeking the Roots of Violence." Where does the balance of argument in each essay lead the reader? Does Flaherty's essay sway the case for social investigation over biological research?

"Seeking the Roots of Violence" by Anastasia Toufexis

This essay works well as a companion to Flaherty's "The Ghetto Made Me Do It" from the same section. Where Flaherty takes up social issues as possible roots of crime and does not touch on genes, Toufexis's subject is genetics. The authors use basically the same journalistic style—informing, weighing the arguments, and ultimately expecting intelligent, moral involvement from the reader. Toufexis does not have the luxury of a specific case based on genetics, but she kicks off with strong contemporary examples and, like Flaherty, uses human interest quotes from researchers.

An interesting omission from Toufexis's work is any mention of the influence of the external environment on the fetus in utero. This could be an additional factor for debate influencing findings, particularly those mentioned in paragraph 8 on identical twins. You could also ask students to research statistics on the background of criminals to find correlating social factors, remembering that, for any factor, correlation doesn't necessarily mean cause.

As in Flaherty's essay, the author's questions themselves provide themes for student work. In addition, it may be useful to set the task of writing an essay using the same approaches to subject, research, and presentation, and with a specific readership in mind.

STUDENT ESSAY: **"Teen Sex: 'Too Scary Out There for Me'"**
by Mari Kinney

Sixteen years old at the time she wrote this, Kinney makes her thesis clear in a straightforward essay supported by narrative on a universal theme. What may be striking, but goes unquestioned by Kinney, is the young age at which dating becomes a serious matter. Is twelve generally a starting point these days and do many teen relationships become as serious as the one described? What does it say about Kinney and her friends that a teenage relationship assumes such importance in their lives? Was it sex that "messed everything up" or the unwillingness to be out of a relationship? Students in any class will probably find much essay material just from the range of responses, from lively to embarrassed, on the subject of teen sex and the questions it raises. Some students may be able to relate similar scenarios and be familiar with the ethnic and religious culture resulting in the girl's exile.

Kinney's essay can be encouraging as it shows what can be achieved without research and without particularly sophisticated language. Students who can match her sincerity and strength of opinion will be off to a good start.

Using Chapter 5: Viewpoints on Culture and Heritage

If the make-up of your class is culturally diverse, consider using this chapter early in the course. As the chapter's introduction states, a great immigration surge to this country—both legal and illegal—has occurred since the 1970s. The United States is now the fifth largest Spanish-speaking country in the world. Soon major cities, such as Los Angeles and Miami, will have more Spanish speakers than English ones. Over twelve million Asians will have immigrated here by the year 2000. The great change in the cultural make-up of our country that is in process makes for a current theme of interest to many students. Set the groundwork for this chapter by referring to the chapter's prefatory comments. Ask students their reactions to the Statue of Liberty, immigrant pictures, and the caption.

The diversity of cultural heritage is reflected in this chapter's reading selections: One discusses the influence of the Latino population on all aspects of our lives; one discusses the "great divide" or the alienation and prejudice that divides American-born Latino children and their immigrant classmates; one recounts a woman's quest for her cultural heritage and where it led her; one discusses the legacy of the Westerinens, or those who are trying to declare themselves descendants of Thomas Jefferson and Sally Hemings; one focuses on "black English"; another narrates the experience of an Armenian growing up in two cultures, to name a few. The student essay, written by a Vietnamese man, describes the hardships of his family's flight to this country.

Cultural heritage makes a rich topic for outside reading. You might want to call for some nonlibrary research, suggesting that students interview family members for more information about their own culture, or interview students on campus from a culture different from their own.
for essays.

"The Legacy of Generation Ñ" by Christy Haubegger

Christy Haubegger is the founder of *Latina* magazine. The authors uses examples in a very compelling way to support her thesis—ask students to list all of these examples that truly support the author's contention that "The United States will be undeniably ours. Again."

Have students look at paragraph 3. Ask students why they think the author finds it necessary to point out that the population growth of Hispanics is driven by a natural increase (births over deaths) rather than immigration. Why is this significant?

It might also be interesting to ask students if they feel the influence of the Hispanic population in their own lives, depending on where you live and teach. Are there Hispanic markets, restaurants, or shopping areas where you and your students live and work? Do students frequent these areas? Why or why not? Are there any other ethnic groups in your area that influence the surroundings as much as Hispanics do in other certain parts of the country? What are these ethnic groups? How do they influence the area in which you live and work, from both a cultural and political standpoint?

This selection can also raise issues regarding bilingual education in the United States. Again, depending on where you live and teach, this may or may not be a "hot button" issue. Paragraph 7 discusses this issue briefly, but really only scratches the surface of the debate. You may want to touch on the issue of bilingual education in class, depending on time and how you think students will react to the discussion. Or, you can have students address the issue in a personal opinion paper as outlined in #3 of "Pursuing Possible Essay Topics."

"The Great Divide" by Michael Quintanilla

Peer group pressure in the educational arena links this essay with Asfahani's "Time to Look and Listen." Both writers focus on the desire for acceptance, and the tensions created by balancing this desire with pride in the home culture. It's worth discussing how Quintanilla, by writing about intraracial segregation, is describing cultural and social phenomenon that underlie racial prejudice as an issue of status. (The essay, "Eggs, Twinkies and Ethnic Stereotypes," by Jeanne Park in the chapter on social concerns, provides further material for exploration of ethnic stereotypes.)

Asfahani and Quintanilla both see value in group sharing of heritage and you may want to try a "storytelling" session both for an increased understanding between students and for inspiration. Demographic statistics, as cited by Quintanilla, are another useful, if deceptively dry, source of themes for student essays on racial trends.

Ask students of different ethnic origins if self-consciousness, image, and self-segregation are still aspects of students' lives at higher levels of learning. Can emotions still be as raw as those experienced by the tearful, eleven-year-old sixth grader quoted in "The Great Divide"? Does the view of American kids "as lazy, unmotivated and disrespectful" prevail? Plenty of material here for fruitful student interaction!

"Cultural Baggage" by Barbara Ehrenreich

Barbara Ehrenreich is a regular contributor to *Ms. Magazine*, and *Mother Jones*, and is known for her left-leaning political views. There are difficult words and phrases used in this selection, but it was included in the new edition because of the questions it raises concerning cultural heritage. Encourage students to stick with the piece, and again, to look up unfamiliar words or to reread passages in order to fully understand what the author is saying.

Many Americans, like the author, are raised with no defined cultural heritage. Many, however, have clearly defined heritages, and define themselves as ____________ -American, depending on their family background. You will probably have a mix of students in your class that fall into these two categories. This article should provide a good basis for discussing the notion of cultural heritage, traditions inherent in having a defined cultural heritage, and the "baggage"—to use Ehrenreich's term—that comes with either having or not having this defined heritage.

If students do not have a clearly-defined heritage, ask them how this has affected them (if it has). What have they done to satisfy "a craving for tradition or roots" (paragraph 4), if they, like the author, have experienced a void? For students who have a clearly-defined heritage, ask if they have enjoyed it throughout their lives? Why or why not? What does it mean to be of that heritage? Has it helped them or been a hindrance? They should be specific in their responses to these questions.

And, finally, what do students think of the advice "Think for yourself; always ask why"? Do they think this is sound advice? If you would like to use this as a writing assignment instead of an in-class discussion question, it is listed as question #4 in the "Pursuing Possible Essay Topics" section.

"Why Must Everything Be Black or White?" by E.R. Shipp

One significant quote in this article may spark some discussion in class. In paragraph 9, the author quotes Sabrina LeBeauf from "The Cosby Show": "Up until 'The Cosby Show,' I don't' think people realized that African-Americans came in all different hues, all different colors from the rainbow…" Her point was that many people felt it was unlikely that such a light-skinned black woman would be the daughter of darker-skinned Cosby. Do students agree or disagree with this statement? Why?

What is E.R. Shipp saying about race in this selection? What makes people more black than white? And what role has history played in perpetuating these distinctions and the categorizing of people in this country according to race?

Students can also discuss how they identify themselves. Do they see themselves as just American, or "Irish-American," "Lebanese-American," or "African-American"? Or does it depend upon what cultural or ethnic group they are in at the time?

Shipp uses the example of the Westerinens to support her thesis. Do students think that the use of this—and the other examples included—is effective? Why or why not?

"Time to Look and Listen" by Magdoline Asfahani

Asfahani's experience of prejudice rooted in misinformation brings her to a mature appreciation of the importance of education and a real acceptance of diversity of heritage.

More than the other essays in this section, "Time to Look and Listen" also raises the issue of religion as part of heritage. Are Judeo-Christian traditions strong among your students and how much do they know or care about other religious beliefs?

Notice the formality of language in this essay (evident, for example, in the first sentence and ones such as "My parents had never said anything even alluding to such sentiments"), demonstrating the care taken by someone striving to be educated. The last two sentences are powerful, but are they grammatically correct? Why have they slipped so easily past an editor's eye?

Asfahani considers herself an American, a nice contrast with Liu Zongren in "After Two years in The Melting Pot" where he reflects that "most of the successful Chinese I had met . . . never thought of themselves as Americans."

There's room for debate here!

"If Black English Isn't a Language, Then Tell Me, What Is?"
by James Baldwin

Here is the essay containing Baldwin's defense of black English as mentioned by Rachel Jones in "What's Wrong with Black English." Here also is a dose of polemics! Baldwin makes several provocative points about American society mainly to be found in his final paragraph. How do students answer these? Does Baldwin find agreement and from which ethnic groups? Does the opinionated, even angry tone, serve to alienate or win his readers?

Baldwin describes black English as a major tool of survival for an entire people, stating that this makes it a language, evolving to help people to "control their circumstances." Is he describing language in this instance or would "code" be a better term? Was "brutal necessity" present in the evolution of standard English, including twentieth-century vocabulary such as "web site" and "disco," and, if so, is there a case to make for recognition and encouragement of speakers of Latin, Greek, and Anglo-Saxon?

Baldwin uses examples of black English finding general, if diluted currency within mainstream English. What other languages inform modern English and how has English infiltrated other tongues?

Of course, Jones's essay is a natural companion piece to Baldwin's. She would probably point out that nowhere in his essay does Baldwin use black English to make his case. He also does not indicate how black English might be used if it were to be officially recognized. Do these points weaken his claim to call black English a language? Students could also debate the role of literature within Baldwin's frame of definition and if he considers the notion of *sharing* cultural aspects as well as controlling them.

As with the Brooks poem, "We Real Cool" in *Chapter 4: Viewpoints on Human Behavior,* recent furor over the implied 1996 recognition in a northern California county school district of "ebonics" as an official language may add some spice to the discussion.

"What's Wrong with Black English" by Rachel L. Jones

A counter argument to Jones can be found in James Baldwin's "If Black English Isn't a Language, Then Tell Me, What Is?" It's worthwhile to read portions of Baldwin's viewpoints to compare with Jones's.

The subject prompts some great discussions, especially if you have some vocal African-Americans in class. Ask: Is there such a thing as "black English"? Is it incorrect to speak black English? Is speaking black English similar to speaking "Spanglish"? Should black English be preserved? Why is there such a phenomenon as black English?

STUDENT ESSAY: **"Coming to America"** by Hieu Huynh

When we have foreign students in our classes, we should take every opportunity to make use of their experiences as a way of broadening both our students' and our own awareness of other cultures. I have found that most Asians are a bit shy about talking in class or discussing anything about themselves, but once made to feel comfortable, they open up and add much to a class.

The student essay in this chapter may not stand as an example of college-level writing, but it reflects much worth discussing: the struggle to escape persecution, the struggle to get to this country, the struggle to survive in a new country, and the struggle to learn a new language. Most of our students have never experienced what this young man has had to deal with. The essay speaks for itself.

Using Chapter 6: Viewpoints on Some Social Concerns

This chapter is intended as an extension of Chapter 5, although it doesn't have to be taught that way. It moves from cultural heritage into social concerns that stem from differing cultural values. In addition to discussing the two brief newspaper reports in the introduction to the chapter, you might want to read the following passage from David Bender's *American Values: Opposing Viewpoints:*

> It is important to consider every variety of opinion in an attempt to determine the truth. Opinions from the mainstream of society should be examined. Also important are opinions that are considered radical, reactionary, minority or stigmatized by some uncomplimentary label. An important lesson of history is the fact that many unpopular and even despised opinions eventually gained a widespread acceptance. The opinions of Socrates, those attributed to Jesus, and Galileo are good examples of this. To have a good grasp on your own viewpoint, you must understand the arguments of those with whom you disagree.

Because this chapter contains differing opinions on social issues, students should be asked to set aside their own biases when they read the essays and discuss the topics brought up in this chapter. Essays included range from opinions on racial and ethnic prejudices to religious concerns.

Go over the definitions of values, norms, and roles provided in the chapter's prefatory comments before assigning any essays in this chapter.

"Ethical Tightrope" by Jim Lichtman

Jim Lichtman poses some serious questions in this selection about ethics. Is it possible to remain ethical in corporate America and our own personal lives. Lichtman takes the stance that we need to commit to a set of standards that are unimpeachable. Do students agree with this stance or do they think that in certain instances it is okay to "fudge" a bit? Why?

Paragraphs 9-13 offer a good example of process in an essay. Point out to students the three things that Lichtman says we should do to return to the standards that we once had a country and ask them for their reactions. Are these standards hard to live by? How do they feel about Lichtman's contention that "Good character is formed by living under conditions that demand good conduct"?

Why do students think that Lichtman uses questions and comments from corporate executives so frequently in this essay? Is it a function of his job as a professional speaker or is he making some kind of comment on corporate America? Why do students feel the way they do about this question?

Students should look particularly at paragraphs 17-26 and decide if they agree with these statements. Can they—or would they even choose—to live their lives according to Lichtman's credo? Why or why not?

"Keeping Faith in Kids" by David Gergen

This article is especially compelling, given the spate of crimes committed by and against teens in recent months. If you have a large number of "teens" (18 and 19 year olds) in your class, this article may spark some debate about how Americans, in general, view "generation Y." If you have a mix of students (some traditionally-aged, some non-traditional), you will still get a great deal of feedback about how teens are viewed in this country, and hopefully your class will let you know if they think this view is justified. The main question to ask is if students agree with the statement in paragraph 3: "this generation is much healthier than the gloomy headlines in recent weeks would suggest." You may want students to discuss this in class, or write an opinion paper either agreeing or disagreeing with the author.

What do students think is the reason for the "extreme antisocial behavior" that exists for some teens? Do they have any ideas on how to combat this feeling? What are some of their suggestions?

It might be helpful to discuss the questions in "Evaluating the Author's Viewpoints" in class or to form small groups to discuss the questions.

"Big Ideas for a Better America" by John F. Kennedy, Jr.

This article was chosen for inclusion in the revision prior to the death of Kennedy, his wife, and sister-in-law in a plane crash near Cape Cod. At the time, the author was the editor of *George Magazine*, and spoke or wrote every now and then about politics and his own political views.

This article, taken from USA Weekend, starts with the question of apathy among young Americans in terms of politics, and then offers solutions to the problem. It might be helpful to discuss the large issue of on-line voting and to ask students what problems (besides those listed in the article) they see inherent in such a plan.

Ask students to respond to the last line of the selection "We need to develop dramatic steps to revitalize our democracy for the next century." Do they agree or disagree? Why? As a class, do they feel apathy towards politics and the voting process? Why? Are any students from countries that are not democratic in nature? What can they bring to this discussion? The more diverse your class is culturally, the more interesting it will be to discuss the apathy that Kennedy discusses in his selection.

"Eggs, Twinkies and Ethnic Stereotypes" by Jeanne Park

Park wrote this piece when she was a junior at Stuyvesant High School. It serves as a model for teaching both the narrative essay form and for dealing with stereotypes at three levels: her own superiority complex, the teacher's belief that all Asians are smart in math, and racial bigotry. Dealing with all the questions under "Looking at Structure and Style" and "Evaluating the Author's Viewpoints" is worth your time.

Some of these issues are very sensitive ones, depending on your class make-up. But why bother teaching composition if the bottom line isn't to get students to deal thoughtfully and intelligently with the very issues Park explores?

"Our Tired, Our Poor, Our Kids" by Anna Quindlen

Yes, this is one of two selections by Anna Quindlen in this text. It was chosen because it puts a different face on the homeless—that of a child. Have students ever thought about the plight of homeless children? Quindlen does an excellent job of showing just how difficult it is to be a homeless child, get an education, and lead a productive life. Hopefully, this selection will be as much of an eye-opener for students as we intend it to be.

How do students feel about the homeless population in general? Are they sympathetic to the struggles that these people face? Why or why not? After reading this selection, are they more or less sympathetic? Again, why?

Discuss the issue of the "parallel universe" that Quindlen presents. Ask students to discuss both ends of the parallel universe. Do they think that Quindlen is making judgments on one or the other, or is she presenting things in a factual, straightforward manner?

This is also a good selection about which to discuss purpose. What was Quindlen's purpose in writing this selection? And, how can you tell? Ask students to pick one sentence from this selection that gives them some clue as to why she wrote the selection.

"Severing the Human Connection" by H. Bruce Miller

Miller's essay raises the issue of honesty and integrity. "Is it that the people are simply incorrigibly dishonest," he asks, "that the glue of integrity and mutual respect that holds society together is finally dissolving?" A good question for us to consider.

I find it interesting to mention to my classes that in my youth we never locked our house or our cars. It was safe for a youngster to ride the city bus alone or walk the streets at night. Storekeepers trusted us to pay the next time if we happened to be short on a purchase. Then I ask why life has changed, and in what direction we seem to be going. Some interesting answers surface.

This selection works well for a discussion of tone, attitude, and style. Point out that the author was prompted to write by his reaction to an ordinary event. Students often overlook such personal incidents and perspectives as possibilities for interesting compositions.

"My God, My Constitution" by Phil Donahue

This selection is a companion piece for the one that follows, "Pledge Words Do No Harm to Nonbelievers" by Rochelle Riley, and should be studied jointly.

Before reading both of these selections, have students say the pledge of allegiance. Does reciting "under God" resonate with them—either in a positive or negative way? Why?

At the time this text was written, Phil Donahue had a talk show on a cable news network. If the show is still on air when the book is published, students should watch either a portion of an episode or an entire episode to see how Donahue comes across. If they do have an opportunity to view Donahue's show, do they think his writing style is indicative of his verbal communication style? If so, how?

Pay particular attention to paragraph 1 of this selection. How does this introduction serve to underscore Donahue's writing style, tone, and opinion on the subject of the Pledge? And, how do students feel about the inclusion of paragraphs 4-6? Is Donahue stating facts or being heavy-handed? Why?

As an argumentative essay, how do students feel about Donahue's style? Is it effective or too blatant? How would they rewrite it to be more effective?

"Pledge Words Do No Harm to Nonbelievers," by Rochelle Riley

Now that they have read both essays, how do students feel about the controversy surrounding the words "under God" in the Pledge?

Students can look at these two essays side by side and decide who presents a better argument, regardless of student's personal feelings about the issue. Does Donahue or Riley present a better argument? Why? Asking this question and looking at the essay is a great collaborative activity for class.

As with the Donahue selection, you can also discuss tone and its effect on the essay's effectiveness.

STUDENT ESSAY: **"Should I Believe in God?"** by Amy Kimoto

Published in the Youth Opinion section of a newspaper, this piece was headed up by a summary: "Do I have to worship the Founding Fathers to believe in the Constitution? One can be moral without religion." This short paragraph neatly sums up Kimoto's views: Are they shared by a minority or majority of students? Kimoto's sense of morals is traditional, but she sees them as underlying, not as a product of religion. Is she typical of modern youth?

It may be worthwhile to investigate what kinds of background relate to different religious views. Kimoto makes no mention of parental views, only of a conventionally religious upbringing, and she produces a bold and confident piece with unconventional conclusions and opinions obviously her own. Discussion might reveal interesting connections between factors such as education, location, and parental influence.

Besides homosexuality, on what other social issues do religions act as moral guardians? How much is belief in God an issue itself in today's largely secular society?

Using Chapter 7: Viewpoints on Family and Relationships

This chapter's theme is broad and significantly familiar to all students. It contains an assortment of writing styles and viewpoints on family and relationships. The introductory comments to the chapter discuss six major qualities shared by healthy families universally. One way to get students interested in the chapter's theme would be to discuss these in class, or have students react to them in a writing exercise as a warm-up before assigning the readings.

Some students may not want to discuss their family relationships, but at the least they can discuss relationships they have had with friends, with persons of the opposite sex, with teachers, co-workers, and so on.

"Silent Bond" by David Biro

You can begin the discussion of this reading by asking students if they have members of their family about whom they know little and why, as discussed by David Biro in chapter 4. How do students feel about the sacrifice that Biro's sister made for him? And his subsequent reaction as described in Paragraph 9?

This selection offers an opportunity to look at descriptive language and word choice, e.g. "languishing marrow," "external data," "a wisp of a memory." Ask students if Biro's choice of words and the story he tells gives them a mental image of him. Why?

Biro uses this narrative to develop his theme of family. Do they students think that his experience brings him any closer to his sister? Why? Why does Biro insert the story of the other transplant patient in paragraph 10. What does this underscore about his relationship with Michelle?

Students can take the opportunity after reading this selection to learn more about the donor program that is referred to in paragraph 10, why someone would need a marrow donation, or the problems inherent in marrow transplants. Any of these topics would provide good research opportunities.

"The Perfect Family" by Alice Hoffman

Thanks to never-ending reruns, students may still be familiar with the happy family format of 1950s television shows. In fact, reruns reveal an interesting progression to the still middle-class, live-at-home college student orientation of "Happy Days," and further on to the clean-living professional single woman (not mother) in "The Mary Tyler Moore Show." What about the "The Waltons" and the 1980s rise of working-class "Roseanne"? What do these shows and their popularity, past or present, show about the preoccupation of American audiences with family values?

The 1990s brought not only movie parodies of "The Brady Bunch," but the modern Calvinism of the television show "Seventh Heaven." Are today's students left confused about "real values" or do they entertain Hoffman's implied definition in her last paragraph?

Hoffman has seen some of the realities behind "the perfect family" of the suburban middle classes and uses these and the topic of neglect to illustrate the unsoundness of judgment on the basis of appearances or material provision. She presents alternative criteria in the same way, using example and illustration. How do Hoffman's criteria and style contrast with those of vote-seeking politicians campaigning on family values?

Hoffman's essay presents a strong defense of single mothers based on her own childhood situation and her mother's work. Would the essay improve if it extended to single men as parents, and so on? Hoffman's implicit conclusion is about the prime importance of love in families: Ask students to consider what some consequences might be if this were supported by society and other judgments were laid aside.

"My Grandmother" by Linda Pastan

Here one woman writes about another, linked by family, but divided by belief. You can pick up the multiple topics in sequence or begin with a broad take on the social issues raised. Ask students for differences of views, and even experience, according to age, religion, ethnicity, and so on. See if sociology students have any international statistics and reports on arranged marriages and any correlations between matriarchal and patriarchal cultures.

Taking the poem apart, students will find a wealth of ideas about relationships to contrast with their own. Lines 5, 6, 12, and 13 show an exchange of love despite the author's implied rejection of her grandmother's teaching. What emotional qualities might the poet have that sees no need on her part to condemn?

The grudge-holding grandmother presents logic-defying attitudes and a melodramatic touch. Readers can picture the effect she created and guess her family's tendency to appeasement of this matriarch. Her powerful reaction suggests underlying fears and unfulfilled dreams related to her own unwilling, youthful compliance—any psychology majors care to comment?

See if students observe the poem's pattern, presenting her characters in single lines, sequencing concepts from line to line, and using punctuation, lines 10 and 17, to mark a beginning, a middle, and an end to her "story."

This grandmother's lesson was unintentional, but was "teacher" a role she tried to fill? Is it typical today and does it apply to grandsons as well as granddaughters?

"Spoiling Our Kids" by Amy Dickinson

The story told here is one that has been told before—kids today just have too much! Based on Dickinson's examples, it would be hard to argue the point. However, do students think that the author makes a strong argument for teaching kids "the quiet pleasure of waiting"? Why or why not?

There are many sentences contained in this selection that could spark a lively discussion, such as any of those in paragraph 3. Do students think that the author is making any sort of indictment against two-career couples, or executive dads? Or, is she just stating facts? This would be a great place to discuss fact and opinion, and using sentences from paragraph 3 could help underscore each concept. After this, spend some time with students on the questions contained in "Evaluating the Author's Viewpoints."

Students can also reflect on their own childhoods and think about what they might do differently with their own children. This is a good topic to explore in a comparison/contrast essay.

"House of Cards" by Kevin Gray

This is a powerful narrative that goes back and forth from the present to the past, when Anthony was alive. Discuss with students this narrative tool and get their reactions to it. Given the arc of the story and the way the author moves the narrative along, it seems to make perfect sense to structure the story in this way. Do students agree? Would the story have the same emotional impact if it had been taught in a more linear way with a description of Anthony's life first and then the story about Chris?

"Evaluating the Author's Viewpoints" explores the stories from many different angles and asks students to get inside Gray's head a little bit. It also asks students to project into the future by asking them if Gray gives any indication of how Chris's life will turn out. Students could write an essay that is set ten or fifteen years in the future in which they explore that question. Where is Chris? How did things turn out for him? Did heredity win out over his personal goals?

You can also discuss the card trick with the students as a metaphorical device. Why does the author include this and how does it work as a device?

"Black Unlike Me" by Jana Wolff

Jana Wolff is the author of "Secret Thoughts of an Adoptive Mother;" this selection originally appeared in the Sunday magazine section of *The New York Times*. This is one of the more difficult selections included in the text, both from the standpoint of writing style, language, and the subject being broached (biracial adoption). The topic alone, however, will provide an opportunity for class discussion about the pros and cons of biracial adoption and will allow students to explore their own feelings about something they may or may not have thought of prior to reading the piece.

Have students address the statement "...Ari's evolution into a proud black man will occur largely outside the walls of our home. And most of his growing, I'm convinced, will happen well beyond the reach of my loving white arms." What do students think the author means by this? Do they agree? Form small groups to discuss the conclusion of the selection.

Students should take time to answer the questions in "Evaluating the Author's Viewpoints," which will help them understand the content of the piece while evaluating the writing style, tone, and message the author is trying to convey.

"Where's Papa?" by David Popenoe

For full debate, set this essay with its natural pair, Judith Stacey's, "The Father Fixation" since the latter was written partly in response to Popenoe's views. Popenoe's premise, "the decline of fatherhood is a major force behind many of the most disturbing problems that plague American society," is stated in paragraph 2. This statement follows an introductory paragraph ending with the heart-tugging extrapolation that over half of America's children are unable "to say goodnight to their dads." Students will see this is typical of Popenoe's use of emotional appeal throughout the piece, e.g., paragraph 3, the word "calamity," paragraph 5, "monumental," paragraph 13, "breathtaking," and so on. How does this reflect on his use of science to support his assertions? By comparison, is Stacey's style more convincing and/or more readable?

Students can pick up Stacey's specific points of opposition to some of Popenoe's opinions and evidence, including, in paragraph 10, his statement that "having an unmarried father is even worse . . . than having a divorced father." Stacey's counter argument comes in paragraph 4. Several issues like this could serve as debating points, but can students bring in any additional data from other classes like sociology and even history? Should debate really be about Stacey's third paragraph, where she casts doubt on much of Popenoe's material and highlights a tendency to present "correlations as though they were causes"?

Is opinion easy to separate from fact and serious theory? How keen is Popenoe to see research leaning in favor of his views? He cites, for instance, paragraph 33, a project that saw men find work when helped to become better fathers; this result was not, apparently, from the men re-establishing two-parent families and so does not align with Popenoe's main hypothesis. How do students themselves defend or find fault with Popenoe's arguments? Discussion in the essay is wide-ranging, and students' own experiences in several areas—for example, their father's role in their emotional development—can be tapped.

"The Father Fixation" by Judith Stacey

One of two professors of sociology with essays in this section, Stacey makes a partial response to the other, David Popenoe. Stacey's is the shorter piece, but both are written for the general reader and use scientific data to support their cases. Stacey's work, as a response, goes further as it undermines the evidence presented in the other. In doing so, it may be useful to students as an example of critique. For suggestions on using the two essays together, see the summary for instructors on Popenoe's piece.

Note the topical opening of "The Father Fixation." The author's contrasting views are presented only after concise analysis and examples designed to expose false premises behind typical "family values" crusades. How current are related issues at the time of reading? Does fatherhood have a high profile and, if so, is it linked at all to an election or perhaps to celebrity—for instance, Bill Cosby writing on the subject, or the birth of children in the British royal family? Students could also review published material for factors involved in earlier eras when the role of fathers was a major topic in society.

Both Popenoe and Stacey attempt to present objective cases. (For a more human contrast in this section students can read Hoffman's, "The Perfect Family" which draws on personal experience rather than statistics or other research.) Part of Stacey's purpose, is to point out the dangers of using "apparently objective language," paragraph 1. Do students find she avoids this flaw herself, and can they find other examples for different issues where quasi-scientific statements are bandied about?

STUDENT ESSAY: **"My Younger Sibling"** by Anne Rushi

Parents, peer groups, celebrities, and teachers—among others—are commonly viewed as role models, but how often is this true for siblings? Rushi believes she would have behaved differently had she been aware of her ability to influence her younger sister. Do students agree? You may want to see how many of them are older brothers or sisters and whether or not they feel a need to moderate their behavior as a result.

What does the essay say about the level of communication in general within families like Rushi's and her boyfriend's? Is it typical and how could it have contributed to the author's need to act "cool" as well as her lack of awareness about her role within the family?

Note the absence of any mention of family values yet their obvious prime importance to both sets of parents. Abortion and contraception are not discussed by Rushi in her essay. The parents of both families cooperate to see their children married and housed. The need to preserve social order seems prime. There are shades of "generation gap" issues here and they may well ring true for several students.

Students could also read the student essay, "Teen Sex: 'Too Scary Out There for Me,'" from the section on human behavior for another angle on the concept of young people coming to a belated mature understanding of their influence and the consequences of actions in general.

On the subject of siblings in particular, students will find a wealth of material in *Born to Rebel* by Frank Sulloway, published by Pantheon, 1996.

Using Chapter 8: Viewpoints on Work

Since many students are presently working or have worked, or are in college preparing for some type of employment, familiarity and interest in the work theme are built in for you. However, if you've been teaching for a long time, you know that many students don't know what type of career for which to prepare, or they have grandiose expectations for future professions they probably will never achieve. This chapter offers students an opportunity to reflect on their work goals.

"What Does Your Color Pen Say About You?" by Jessie Milligan

If you've tackled the chapters of this text in order, the students have explored some very serious topics. This selection is a break from all of that—by discussing the not-so-serious topic of pen color and its relation to job performance.

Have students read the selection and discuss the merits of the survey discussed in this selection. Do they think it has merit? Why or why not? Do they think that job performance can be determined or evaluated based on information like this?

Take an informal survey in class about the pen colors that your students prefer. Have students evaluate the findings and compare the personalities and work habits of individual students to those found in the Pilot survey.

This will be a fun way to discuss the concept of validity. Have students write a summary of the findings and whether or not they think the Pilot survey has any merit, based on the outcome of the class survey.

When they have finished that exercise, students can explore some of the topics in "Pursuing Possible Essay Topics."

"On a Role" by Lamar Graham

From its punning title on, Graham's piece is keenly aimed at a specific audience. Information about the future job market for young people is presented in a pacey, casual style, well suited to its original publication in *Rolling Stone*. The author's journalistic technique, which strings together quotes from experts and wraps them around other "dry" information, can be compared with the essays by Flaherty and Toufexis in the chapter on human behavior.

Graham has selected some pretty meaty quotes. You might want to cover the way he uses quoted material from the same source under different headings, often having to almost fully reiterate acknowledgments to remind us who is speaking. It could be useful to trace back from the organization of the essay to the probable way it was researched in terms of deciding on sources and then gathering and sorting information.

Graham writes "America will end up gaining more than 17.7 million jobs. Er, roles." Does this kind of semihumorous tone distract from the major points of the article or does it help to get them across? There is some similarity, here, to Stanat's "How to Take a Job Interview" from the same chapter. What assumptions do the authors make about students as readers?

The subject itself presents an obvious opportunity for discussion about students' plans for higher education and work. How many budding funeral directors versus "adventure travel entrepreneurs" are there in class? In view of their own skills and aims, does Graham's essay discourage or offer hope? Is the author's list of employment categories (medicine, technology, management, education, and recreation) as broad as it could be?

Graham touches on the value of a liberal arts degree. You can make a cross-chapter connection on this topic with "The Practicality of the Liberal Arts Major" by Sikes and Murray from the chapter on learning. Do Graham's broader essay and different sources actually present a better case and, if so, why?

"For a Lady I Know" by Countee Cullen

Like Gwendolyn Brooks' poem, "We Real Cool," Cullen has crafted a short, yet effective poem about the issues of class, race, and work in America. Have students take turns reading the poem aloud, and listen for differences in intonation and style.

Ask students to identify the different themes of the poem and the issues raised. For a homework assignment, you could ask students to go on the internet and do some additional research about Countee Cullen and the poem. When was it written? What was going on at the time that would influence the author to write this poem?

Students can also either discuss or write about the "Lady." Who is she? Where does she come from? Why does she feel that "poor black cherubs" should "rise at seven To celestial chores?"

Although this poem is perfect for in-class discussion, it also provides a wealth of opportunity for good writing assignments. Students can write a personal response to the poem or discuss the larger issues of race and class in an essay.

"Women Still Fighting for Job Equality" by DeWayne Wickham

DeWayne Wickham writes for the "Opinion" section of *USA Today*. This selection provides you with an opportunity to discuss the concept of the "glass ceiling," a term with which students may or may not be familiar. Ask students if they knew what the term was before reading the selection, and if not, if they now know what it means from the context of the reading.

The author uses quotes throughout the selection to support his thesis. Students can discuss if they think these quotes from Diane Fischer (the first-time boxing promoter) and Elizabeth Toledo (Vice President of NOW) are effective tools in developing and supporting the author's thesis.

It would be interesting to have students pick an essay from the "Pursuing Possible Essay Topics Section" to get a sense of whether or not they agree with the author about sexism in the workforce. You can also have students form small groups for in-class discussion about the topic of sexism and the concept of the glass ceiling.

"My Mother Never Worked" by Bonnie Smith-Yackel

The structure of this essay is worth pointing out to students. It opens and closes with a conversation between the author and someone in the Social Security Office. The opening conversation establishes the mother's death through the author's request for a death-benefit check. While she is on hold, the author reminisces in a kind of flashback on her mother's long and arduous life. When the Social Security clerk gets back on the line to explain that there will be no death-benefit check because the mother "never worked," we feel the irony of the situation.

All the questions under "Looking at Structure and Style" are useful for discussion of the essay's structure.

"The Company Man" by Ellen Goodman

Goodman, as social commentator, tells a simple tale of an American life and laces it with deadly irony. The essay focuses on the obsessive work of a male executive and supplies an interesting contrast with "My Mother Never Worked" by Smith-Yackel in the same chapter. Smith-Yackel's female subject works endlessly, but is always at the center of her family. Irony is reserved for the end and the title, whereas Goodman's use of irony supports her intention to create a mood of bitterness about her company man. Do students feel Goodman's story is a true one?

By including cameos of the bitter executive's wife and distanced children, Goodman does an excellent job of conveying the empty emotional results of obsessive work. Society and the workplace in this narrative condone and literally promote self-destructive behavior. Do students feel this is a realistic portrayal and why? Michael Scofield, in "Off the Ladder," takes a very different career approach that might provide students with some useful comparisons.

A summary of emotional hardships of the affluent underlies Goodman's story. This aspect can be tied to essays from the chapter on family relationships. Which evokes the most student feeling—the physical hardships endured by the *working* class in Hoffman's "The Perfect Family" and "A Thanksgiving Celebration" by Nicholasa Mohr, or the individual isolation of the wealthy explored by Ellen Goodman?

The workaholic is a twentieth-century character type, but how far back does the American tradition of business as first priority go?

You could suggest students also research the work ethos of other cultures such as Japan and Jamaica to view alongside Goodman's American example. Have some fun with short personality-type testing in class and use the results to predict consequences in imagined scenarios involving work.

"What Does Sex/Gender Have to Do with Your Job?" by Jeffrey Bernbach

Bernbach's piece is an extract from his 1996 book *Job Discrimination: How to Fight, How to Win*. His prime intent is education and this is served by using the writing patterns of illustration-example, analysis, and definition. Do students anticipate that sexual discrimination will block their career paths in any particular fields and, if so, does this deter them? Do they feel Gingrich's views, no matter how "skewed," are in fact typical? You could ask if some women hold an equally condescending and discriminatory view about men.

What are the implications if an important politician holds discriminatory opinions? What does it say about society that the Title VII antidiscrimination legislation was enacted only thirty years ago? Female astronauts are a very visible symbol for NASA to flaunt; are students also aware of the controversy surrounding the lower profile issue of admission of female cadets to military school in recent years? Is change usually signaled from the top of organizations?

History majors may have information about the notion of "separate spheres" for men and women that developed in the nineteenth century with the advent of industrialization. This could predict less sexual discrimination in modern agrarian societies, and students might want to make a comparative study the basis for their own essays.

"If You Let Me Play…" by Mary Brophy Marcus

This selection provides an interesting counterpoint to Bernbach's in that it discusses the relationship between sports and corporate success for women. Rather than looking at sexual discrimination and gender as a problem for women, it shows through anecdotal information and example how women have succeeded in the workplace through their participation in team sports.

Ask students if they are familiar with Title IX, and what, if anything, they think about the fact that women's sports required a mandate in order to become equal with men's sports in terms of funding. Is this surprising? Why or why not? If you have returning students, perhaps they can share any personal reflections on life either before or after Title IX and any effects the mandate may have had in their lives.

It may be interesting to have a discussion with students about what they feel are the most important benefits they think women derive from participating in team sports. Do they agree with the ones listed in the article? Would reading this selection make them more inclined to get their daughters involved in sports, knowing that they might have a better chance of succeeding in corporate America? Do they think that men derive the same benefits from participating in team sports? Why or why not?

STUDENT ESSAY: **"'Oh, I'm Just a Housewife'"** by Roy Wilson

Wilson says the idea for his essay came from reading Bonnie Smith-Yackel's piece, "My Mother Never Worked." It made him take another look at his mother's typical day. While he had always appreciated everything his mother had done for him and his family, Wilson says the Smith-Yackel essay caused him to get more in touch with his own mother and the work she does every day.

The short essay is a tribute of sorts to housewives like his mother. His title attracts our attention and his opening paragraph makes his viewpoint clear. His paragraphs are coherent and he supports them with specifics.

During class discussion, however, some students have trouble focusing on Wilson's actual thesis statement when he shares his essay in class. Some students point out that the opening paragraph raises the question of why so many housewives think of themselves as "just" housewives. But the second paragraph, they say, raises a whole series of questions of "why?" Has the male caused this? Has society? Who is to blame for this?

In the next paragraph, a few students feel that Wilson forgets his own questions as he begins to wonder what would happen if housewives went on strike. They like the way the paragraph describes what would happen, but feel that the questions in paragraph 2 still hasn't been addressed. See if your students feel the same.

In paragraph 4, Wilson shows us what would happen if the male tries to assume the housewife's role. While his descriptions of the chaos are clear and humorous, Wilson's critics feel he still has not addressed his own questions.

Wilson ends by saying he doesn't think males will take over, in essence because they can't handle the job. Then he calls for a national holiday for housewives.

While everything Wilson says certainly centers around his subject, the essay seems loose and disjointed to some. They can't understand what specific point Wilson wants to make. If his point is to develop the idea that housewives are "Wonder Women," then they feel he needs to provide more examples of why housewives deserve such praise and give less attention to the male's attempts at housework.

Other students in the class, however, feel that although Wilson's essay is not tightly held together, he does imply that a housewife should be considered a Wonder Woman by showing the male's awareness that he wouldn't want the job. They feel his critics were being too picky for the type of essay Wilson wrote.

What do your students think? What advice would they give to Wilson?

Using Chapter 9: Viewpoints on the Media

Many students are unaware of the media's influence on our thinking and values, so you may want to give some emphasis to the theme. Several informative books mentioned in the chapter's preface are useful references for you or for student research projects. In addition, many of the items under the section "Pursuing Possible Essay Topics" contain leads to sources on various aspects of the media. Given the extraordinary power of the television medium, the essays in this chapter lean more in that direction.

Because most students have grown up with television as a natural part of their environment, they seldom evaluate what they have grown accustomed to seeing. As an eye opener of sorts for students, I play back in class a videotaped broadcast of the national evening news from the night before. I then have the students count the number of commercials, keep track of the actual amount of time devoted to news, note what news is emphasized, and evaluate the style of the commentators. This sometimes requires running portions of the tape more than once. For some students, this is the first time they have watched the news; for others, it gives them new viewing eyes.

I also play back some commercials, discussing the audience for whom they are intended, the honesty and values being displayed, the need for the product, and the quality of the presentation. Try turning off the monitor and have students listen to the news without the video portion. Is there much difference? Such activities create some interest in the media theme.

You can also ask students to bring in a particular edition of a newspaper. Go through the paper with them, looking at the attention given to hard news as opposed to the space devoted to such features as advice columns, movie reviews, garden ideas, recipes, advertisements, and other non-news. Take this opportunity to point out the editorial section, letters to the editor, syndicated columnists, and essay contributions. For some students, it's a revelation to discover that essays appear in places outside of textbooks.

You might wish to compare the depth of news coverage presented in the newspaper with that on the news videotape, especially if they both deal with the same day's news. As a way to tease students, ask them why sports coverage gets a section of its own. Why isn't sports coverage included in the business section, since professional sports is really big business? What does such an emphasis on sports say about our values?

Ask students to compare some news magazines, such as *TIME* and *Newsweek.* Or, bring in some copies of *Harper's, Atlantic Monthly, Utne Reader,* or *The New Republic,* for example, to expose students to magazines they may not find at the checkout counters. This may also be an appropriate time to look at the sources for the essays in *Viewpoints* by reading the acknowledgments.

"Calling the C-Word the C-Word" by James Poniewozik

Poniewozik is a regular contributor to Time Magazine and writes about issues in media and entertainment. This is a rather difficult reading, but if students can spend some time on it, they will have plenty to discuss in class and write about when it comes time to craft essays. You may need to explain to students who Coleen Rowley is (paragraphs 17-18) in order for them to understand the concluding context of Poniewozik's argument.

Discuss the author's tone. By opening the selection with "Three cheers for Dennis Pluchinsky," he sets the tone for the essay. Can students recognize the author's tone by this sentence? And, where else in the essay—through the author's choice of words and/or phrases is Poniewozik's tone evident and blatant?

Discuss with students the subject of censorship. Like Pluchinsky, do they think that there is a time and/or place in which invoking censorship is necessary? Why? Or, do they agree with Poniewozik? Why? Students should think carefully about the issue and the ramifications of agreeing with either Pluchinsky or Poniewozik.

Time permitting, students could spend time researching the topic of censorship in order to ask the questions posed in the previous paragraph. In the wake of the terrorists attacks or September 2001, the idea of censoring the media has taken on new elements. Have students think about the idea of censorship in our new environment and ask them to explore if their thinking has changed as a result.

"The Issue Isn't Sex, It's Violence" by Caryl Rivers

Rivers' essay touches on the negative effects of some rock lyrics. With the advent of MTV, rock videos now bring the lyrics to life. Her argument that some rock lyrics incite listeners to violence is not new. But unlike those who call for censorship, Rivers provides her own solution to what she sees as a problem (see paragraph 15 especially). In this piece, written for the *Boston Globe,* Rivers uses several paragraphs to define the problem and present her view, always anticipating those who may disagree with her by presenting and refuting counterarguments.

Some students who disagree with Rivers fail to really examine her arguments because their own bias prevents them from accepting what she presents. Naturally, they don't have to agree with her, but a careful look at her arguments, how she orders and presents them, is worth some class time as an exercise in understanding the argumentative essay. Students may want to know her credentials. Rivers is a professor of journalism at Boston University, a novelist, and frequent essay contributor to newspapers and magazines.

"Trauma TV" by Andrew Ferguson

Andrew Ferguson is a frequent contributor to *TV Guide* and wrote this article in the wake of the plane crash of John F. Kennedy, Jr., his wife, and sister-in-law. Although this is a rather lengthy and difficult selection, it raises some serious questions about media coverage, the right to privacy, and the role of television in our lives.

Hopefully, students will have seen some of the coverage of this tragedy and will be able to contribute to the discussion about the issues raised in the article. If not, perhaps you can have students think about other tragedies that have resulted in massive media coverage—Princess Diana's death or the massacre at Columbine, to name two—to see if they have any opinions about how the media should cover such events. Are these events so newsworthy as to warrant twenty-four hour a day coverage, or should the news be reported without the constant commentary of "certified 'experts'" (paragraph 10)?

Ask students how effective they think it is to open the story with a personal anecdote? Does this help establish the author's tone for the selection? Why or why not?

Students can discuss the question "Can TV do anything without overdoing it?" and perhaps write a personal opinion piece exploring their feelings about this question.

"Pandora's Idiot Box" by David Rakoff

David Rakoff is a writer who lives in New York City and who wrote this article for *The New York Times* Sunday magazine section. The first thing you may want to ask students is why the author titles the piece "Pandora's Idiot Box." They may want to do some quick research in order to find out how Pandora was and why this is significant in the title.

Although the author uses humor and popular culture examples to make his point, ask students if they think there is a serious message in this selection. They can look at paragraph 5 for help and discuss whether or not they agree with the author that "television is thankfully not the only game in town."

Why does the author use so many popular culture references to make his point? Is this effective?

Ultimately, what message is the author trying to convey? Does he do this effectively?

"Summer Kidnapping Panic" by Michelle Goldberg

At the time this text was revised, there seemed to be a spate of kidnappings of children across the United States. The fact at the time, however, was that kidnapping was at a lower level than in the past—a fact that was left out of media coverage of these tragedies.

Although the topic of the kidnappings was topical in the summer of 2002, the issue is much larger. Does the media spend too much time covering tragedies and instilling fear in the hearts of average Americans? Why do students think that that is the case? Or, do students think that the media should react to stories just as it had been—the fear it produces being a necessary byproduct of the reporting?

Having read the opening paragraphs of this selection, were students surprised by the contradictory information presented in paragraph 3? Do they think that the way the author opened the selection was effective? Why or why not?

This is a good selection to discuss the issue of testimony in essay writing. The author uses quotes from private investigators, FBI agents, and authors who specialize in the topic of child kidnappings to support her thesis. Discuss why, in this instance, it is effective. Do students see how using these quotations bolsters her thesis? This and other questions related to this reading are explored in "Looking at Structure and Style."

"Chips Ahoy" by Richard Zoglin

This densely packed essay draws on many different sources (its original publication acknowledged the reporting of several journalists in different locations) as it covers the V chip and a range of issues that surround it. "Filters Can't Block Out the World," by Terry Schwadron in the same chapter takes a broader if shallower look at current censorship tools in general. For a full discussion on censorship of electronic media, set the two essays together.

Interestingly, both writers express major reservations about censorship: Schwadron prefers to rely on "the teaching of values through guidance" so that children themselves can decide what "doesn't fit in their lives"; Zoglin agrees that "sheltering kids . . . is largely futile" and fears the blocking of cartoons could lose a chance for children to "engage in playful fantasy." Do students sympathize with these kinds of views, and do they win out in class debate on media censorship?

"Chips Ahoy" also questions the premises for concern about violence on television and points out how the V chip program cannot be a comprehensive answer. He quotes findings from various surveys, and discusses the difficulties involved in creating systems for rating shows. Topics
from the political popularity of the V chip to the objections of network stations, and the criteria for surveying television could all serve as essay material.

Zoglin's essay also brings up the point that successive generations have survived the pop culture of different eras. Does current pop culture hold any special dangers?

"Filters Can't Block Out the World" by Terry Schwadron

Here's an essay that argues for the responsibilities of parents rather than the imposition of censorship. Schwadron holds a view not often heard that children are capable of deciding for themselves—given the necessary guidance. Note how his summary of parental help is not a black-and-white description of good and evil. He relies instead on teaching values, using "painful discussion" to "hone" "sensitivities" in his children.

Have any students experienced this kind of guidance? Why would it be difficult to rely on this approach in those households, for example, where the television is used as a surrogate baby sitter? Schwadron's argument is also an answer to Caryl Rivers and her essay in this chapter, "The Issue Isn't Sex, It's Violence." Again, though, there is the issue of absent, irresponsible, or indifferent parents. Students could discuss what kind of social measures might be needed to help parents feel as confident as the writer about guiding their children. In the meantime, would some censorship be needed, and would the methods outlined actually work?

Zoglin's essay, "Chips Ahoy," narrows in on V chips as a censorship tool against violence on television. Do students feel Schwadron's proposal is strong enough to counter all the data covered by Zoglin on televised violence?

Schwadron concentrates on censorship of the Internet. What special difficulties relate to computers rather than television? How are the two media different and why does this affect methods of censorship? Do students feel the censorship measures being considered for the Internet are merited or not? Is filtering the Internet a fundamentally more important issue than censoring television because it affects the free speech of many more individuals? Is television content a higher priority to address because it is available to an even larger number of people? See also the notes on Zoglin's essay for further ideas on using the two essays together.

STUDENT ESSAY: **"TV News: Journalism or Propaganda?"** by Jim Stone

This final revision of Stone's essay shows his attention to some basic composition guidelines: a clear thesis, strong support, good paragraph control, sentence variety, helpful transitions, and attention to word choices.

Notice in the first paragraph that Stone makes it clear what his subject and thesis are. Although television stations may begin with the intention of truthfully covering news stories, pressures from various sources, including time itself, may all serve to slant a story by the time we see it on television.

His second paragraph begins, "Here's how it typically works." From there through paragraph 4, Stone takes us from the step-by-step process of reporters covering a news story to the editorial room where the selection of what will be finally shown is decided. As he describes the process, he is also supporting his thesis by showing how and why a story may become slanted by the time we view it on television.

Paragraphs 5 and 6 deal with the editor. Paragraph 5 gives the editor credit for the job he must perform. It recognizes the service the editor provides for us and lets us know that Stone is not accusing all editors of slanting news stories. Paragraph 6, in contrast, shows the disservice an editor can perform when his biases interfere with a story.

It could be argued that paragraph 7 is not needed because it begins to raise a different issue. Stone's topic sentence (that television plays a huge role in who will get elected) is certainly true, but that in itself seems a thesis of its own needing further development and discussion. The previous paragraph (6) ends with a commentary on how editors may slant stories to favor or downplay a political candidate. No doubt that statement brought up the ideas Stone expresses in paragraph 7. But as written, the paragraph takes us away from the process involved in developing a television news story. It doesn't support Stone's thesis.

The last paragraph draws a logical conclusion: We shouldn't believe everything we see and hear on television news. The body of his essay shows us why.

Despite the question of the appropriateness of paragraph 7, Stone's essay shows he applied what he has learned about composition. He began writing with the idea he would compare and contrast the way newspapers report a story with the way television does. As you can see, he narrowed the topic down to something more manageable. After several false starts and many revisions, this student finished with an acceptable essay that fits the assignment.

Using Chapter 10: Opposing Viewpoints on the Death Penalty

This chapter can be used as a type of casebook on capital punishment. Students will have little trouble researching the topic if you wish to have them broaden their information base beyond the arguments here. Two essays argue for capital punishment, two argue against, and one provides an observation of a hanging, although subjective intimations are evident.

During the preparation of this edition, Florida carried out the death penalty through electrocution. Observers witnessed the head of the prisoner burst into flames, causing an outcry against cruel and unusual punishment. Such incidents continue to bring the subject of capital punishment to our consciousness. You might ask your students to research what states carry out capital punishment and how it is done.

"Death Penalty Saves Lives" by Jeff Jacoby

Jeff Jacoby is a writer for the Boston Globe. Have students read this article, paying close attention to the statistics that he uses to support his point. How does this compare with the numerous examples that Koch uses to lay out his argument for the death penalty? Jacoby looks at the issue of the death penalty primarily through the use of numbers—the number of murders committed, the number of executions. This is supported by his statement "...perhaps murder becomes more attractive when potential killers know that prison is the worst outcome they can face." Although Koch agrees with Jacoby's premise, he takes a different approach by discussing the value of human life in paragraph 10 of his selection. It is interesting to look at these pro arguments in the context of how each is presented and compare and contrast arguments for effectiveness based on students' own viewpoints.

Have students read paragraphs 11-12. How do they feel about Jacoby's argument that "Those who call for a moratorium on executions should be calling just as vehemently for a moratorium on prison terms. Why don't they?" It may or may not be obvious that Jacoby believes this, but in the context of this paragraph, is this argument compelling and sound? Why or why not? Although he goes on in paragraph 13 to refute this argument, it is still worth discussing whether or not Jacoby makes a sound argument for the death penalty and how his argument compares to Koch's, particularly paragraph 11, which explores the same aspect of the argument. Which author presents a better argument here and why?

After reading all of the death penalty selections in this chapter, both pro and con, have students discuss the topic and the soundness of the arguments presented in these selections. As before, ask students if they have changed their minds on the topic based on their reading, or are they more convinced of their own viewpoint?

"Death and Justice" by Edward I. Koch

As noted under the comments for Royko's essay, Koch takes six arguments usually presented in opposition of capital punishment and examines them through counterarguments. At many points, he seems to be using "facts" to prove his points. Have students look carefully at Koch's arguments and ask them if they satisfactorily dismiss the arguments against the death penalty.

Koch raises the question of responsibility that comes with law enforcement (paragraphs 13–16). Students who tend to be disinterested in the issue of capital punishment as something too far removed from their own lives can be drawn into the conversation with more interest when discussion turns to their own responsibility in law enforcement.

"Casting the First Stone" by Lloyd Steffen

Steffen's premise is that capital punishment is a "moral problem" not just a social policy fulfilling an American "sense of justice and fair play." Steffen couches his theme in biblical terms, deliberately occupying ground not usually considered liberal territory. Students might care to see where other biblical concepts are used in the various essays in this chapter. Koch, in "Death and Justice," paragraph 6, for example, cites one of the Ten Commandments. In general, is the bible more often a source for proponents or opponents of the death penalty? Does the division in class of pros and antis correlate at all with religious beliefs?

As a long analysis of one main argument using few, but key, illustrations and examples, is Steffen's essay more or less persuasive than those that tackle a greater number of questions?

Steffen pins much of his argument on the case of Richardson in Florida. Are students satisfied with Steffen's assertion that this miscarriage of justice shows the lack of "moral certainty" that must be required of any agency ordering capital punishment? Even more fundamental, do students agree that this moral certainty is essential?

Paragraph 5 takes up the issue of executions performed in faraway places. You could find out if students share the "moral outrage" mentioned by Steffen. Does it extend to the death penalty in America and if not, why not? Is the notion of American "moral superiority" widely believed by students, and does this essay shake the views of any believers?

"Death Penalty's False Promise" by Anna Quindlen

Quindlen opposes the death penalty but confesses that if a loved one of hers were murdered, although she would feel that urge for revenge, she believes at her rational level that such an emotional response is wrong. Quindlen makes several references to Ted Bundy, the handsome young man who was finally caught and convicted for the murder of several young women in many states. She even says that had she been in the wrong place at the right time, she could have been one of Bundy's victims. She admits that had her daughter been one of his victims, she would "with the greatest of pleasure" kill him herself. She gets rather graphic in paragraph 9 when she describes the gruesome killing of six-year-old Adam Walsh. Despite the horrors committed by some people, Quindlen opposes the death penalty to punish them. You will no doubt want to point out to students that this is a good writing technique: It lets her readers know she shares the same emotions as those who favor capital punishment, but she feels it is "stooping to the level of the killers" (paragraph 10).

"A Hanging" by George Orwell

Unlike the other essays in Part II, Orwell's contains little direct commentary, yet he manages through his descriptions to express his feelings toward capital punishment. Because most of us would rather not think about the subject, we tend to let others deal with it. Orwell's essay provides a great contrast. You may want to assign this essay before the others as an attention-getter for the subject.

Have students discuss each witness's reaction to the hanging. Point out the difference in the way each views the hanging: the stoic prisoner; Francis, the head jailer; the fawning "hangman"; the stern, impatient Superintendent; the Eurasian boy; Orwell himself; even the dog. Raise the issue of carrying out your duty, even though it may be a task you morally oppose. You may want to venture into discussion of whether or not one country has the right to impose its morals and laws on another country, which is what is taking place in this essay.

Above all, look closely at the description used.

STUDENT ESSAY: **"Stop Executing Juveniles"** by Trisha Toyota

Toyota's essay does fit the assignment on writing about a controversial issue. Her slant is also a bit different in that she deals with one aspect of the death penalty, lawful juvenile executions. She has attempted to make the topic her own. She also takes a stance and makes her thesis clear. Those are things I like.

But there are some problems for me as a reader. First, her main source seems to be from "a recent editorial" in the *Mobil Register* by Tanya Coke. No date is given so I have no idea how recent this information is. Paragraph 2 is basically Coke speaking, not Trisha. That might pass, but paragraph 3 brings in statistics with no mention of their source. Are they again from Coke's editorial? The last sentence of that paragraph is also a rather sweeping statement. Does the poll taken in Georgia suggest the rest of the country would feel the same way?

I like paragraph 4. It attempts to answer a question readers would ask at this point. The author gives her viewpoints, not someone else's comments. I feel the writer at work here. But paragraph 5 brings in quotes from Victor Strieb. While we are told who he is, what is the source for these quotes? What else has Trisha read? Is this from the editorial mentioned earlier in the essay?

When I read the last sentence, "We must stop letting our courts send children to the executioner," I understand her viewpoint. It is a strong statement of position, but somehow it rings hollow. I'm left with the feeling that this essay was done because it was assigned, not because the author had any real passion for the topic. I'm not saying she doesn't, and I have no way of knowing. I'm simply saying that while the thesis and form of an essay are here, the way the essay is written contains more of the thinking and information of others than it does the writer's thinking and feeling.